INDIAN AND WHITE

INDIAN
AND
WHITE

Sixteen Eclogues

Winston Weathers

UNIVERSITY OF NEBRASKA PRESS
LINCOLN

Acknowledgments of copyrighted material appear
on pages ix–x

For Mother and Inalea

Contents

Acknowledgments

Grateful acknowledgment is made to the following quarterlies, in which the selections listed first appeared:

Cimarron Review, March, 1969, for "Persimmon Wine," which is reprinted by permission of the Board of Regents for the Oklahoma State University.

Arizona Quarterly, Summer, 1950, for "Hills That Are Not Easy," copyright 1950 by the Arizona Quarterly; Winter, 1951, for "Interlude for Christmas," copyright 1951 by the Arizona Quarterly; Winter, 1948, for "Tse'Cabe," "Death of a Choctaw," and "Last Chief of the Comanches," which originally appeared as "Three Indian Tales," copyright 1948 by the Arizona Quarterly; and Spring, 1950, for "The Old Guitars Are Singing," copyright 1950 by the Arizona Quarterly.

Prairie Schooner, Fall, 1946, for "Hound-Dogs Are Calling," copyright 1946 by the University of Nebraska Press; Fall, 1948, for "Pah-se-to-pah," copyright 1948 by the University of Nebraska Press; Spring, 1949, for "Peyote," copyright 1949 by the University of Nebraska Press; Summer, 1949, for "Wah-kon-tah-och-kee-ah: He Talked with God," copyright 1949 by the University of Nebraska Press; and Summer, 1950, for "The Rite of the Chiefs," copyright 1950 by the University of Nebraska Press.

Minnesota Quarterly, Spring, 1950, for "Cibola."

Arlington Quarterly, Summer, 1969, for "Red River."

Introduction

Eclogues are not a common literary form, and perhaps a word of explanation should be made concerning the provenience of the particular eclogues presented in this book. In classical Greece, an eclogue was simply a "selection," a simple piece of literary composition; after Vergil and the use of the term in connection with his pastoral poems, the eclogue became a highly formalized genre with definite idyllic conventions—shepherds and shepherdesses as characters engaged in singing matches, eulogies, and dialogues—the best demonstration in English literature being *The Shepheardes Calender* by Edmund Spenser. In choosing the word "eclogue" to describe my own "selections," I have—I must admit—ignored a good part of its idyllic tradition; rather I have chosen the word simply to suggest a lyric and poetic approach to certain subjects, to suggest a nonurban content, and to avoid calling my work "poems" or "stories" either one.

I began the composition of my eclogues over twenty-five years ago ; they have been written during that long stretch of time in a continuing attempt to preserve in words my private and personal response to the history, legend, personality, and people of the region in which I have actually and imaginatively lived : the southwestern United States, from the northeastern corner of Oklahoma to the bright border of southern Texas. In these eclogues I have dealt with dualities : I've written about two peoples—Indian and white ; about two areas—Oklahoma and Texas ; about two periods of time—present and past. And though I have not consciously so intended, my theme has consistently been "the passage of time," "the alteration of place," "the having had and now the loss."

In their totality, the sixteen eclogues presented here describe something of a journey on the part of a narrator—white, pastoral-oriented, sometimes called "Oflaggerty's Child"—a journey out from the immediate area of the Osage hills (those hills of northern Oklahoma that embrace the Osage nation and where the capital town of Pawhuska, my birthplace, quietly nestles), out among other Indian tribes in Oklahoma, on south into Texas, and then home again, a journey that affects the narrator by making him aware, in a process of maturation, of the mutability of cultures (both Indian and white) and of man's mutability in general. The narrator discovers in Southwestern history and legend, and in the Southwestern scene, certain universal truths—the lessons of life and death, and the common humanity of which we are a part. He makes his "discovery" through obvious and basic experiences involving the human spirit whether that spirit be manifest in an Osage Indian chief, in an Oklahoma rancher, or in a Texas pioneer.

In dealing with regional and cultural material, I have not written as scholar or scientist—though I acknowledge the importance of such disciplines as ethnology, history, anthropology, sociology. My desire, rather, has been to write *as a poet* in an area where particular academic disciplines are too frequently considered the only interpreters. Using three themes— Indian legend, character, and history; the white man's penetration of the American Southwest; and the sensibility of the modern white man as he observes a vanishing and fading world—I have tried to formalize images, personalities, and incidents into poetic patterns held together by a common music: my own sense of metaphor, my own sense of poetic language. I have tried to reify some portion of the Southwestern mystique within a single poetic synthesis.

In making such poetry, my goal has been to give to the legends, anecdotes, historical events, as well as my own observations of Indian and frontier culture, a literary finish that will help them reach an appreciative audience and will contribute to their preservation from a loss that is imminent.

And there is a loss: As we all know much of Indian culture is rapidly disappearing; it deserves some celebration in art in addition to documentation in scholarship. Also the pioneer, frontier world that existed in the Southwest up until very recent times is fading, too, and its disappearance relates to the Indian disappearance; it is all a vanishing of old innocence and old beauty. What remains —as a shining new skyscraper industrial world rises up over the hills and prairies—

is a nostalgia, a nostalgia that I have tried to suggest in the first eclogue of this book, a nostalgia that takes comfort in the magic of re-creative art, its dancing and its wine.

The eclogues are of varying genesis. The first three, "Persimmon Wine," "Hills That Are Not Easy," and "Interlude for Christmas," are re-creations on my part of a world in which I have lived and of the spirit of a region I have known tremendously well. If these eclogues are in any way "winterish" it is because I came into the Osage on a cold Christmas day, confronting life for the first time in a small pink frame house at the foot of one of the steep hills in Pawhuska (the town of Chief White Hair); perhaps the wind and snow blowing in from the plains of Kansas left their mark upon me.

All the Indian tales, from "Tse'Cabe" through "Last Chief of the Comanches," are based upon authentic historical material, upon legends circulating as oral material in my region, or upon my own firsthand encounter with the personalities: I have looked upon the face of such a great chief as Pah-se-to-pah (who rode in the great parades along Ki-he-kah Street) and such a notorious personality as John Stink (who came down to the fence along Skyline Drive when we rode by in a Model A Ford on Sunday afternoons), and I have sat, front row center, at many an Osage Indian dance out in Indian Village on the northeast corner of Pawhuska. Some of the eclogues are obviously based upon information acquired from others—stories told me, data buried in nineteenth-century reports of the Bureau of Indian Affairs, data in publications of limited circulation shelved away in various Indian collections in Oklahoma libraries.

Of the Indian pieces, "Tse'Cabe" and "The Rite of the Chiefs" are legends recorded by nineteenth-century visitors among the Osage; "Wah-kon-tah-och-kee-ah" is a poetized portrait of an actual nineteenth-century personality; "Death of a Choctaw" deals with the actual mode of early Choctaw justice; "Peyote" is a telling of the ritual and religion based upon peyote-taking that flourishes still today among many Indian tribes; "Last Chief of the Comanches" is a famous true story of Quanah Parker, though I have tried to give a special emphasis to the humanity of this particular Indian-and-white situation.

"The Old Guitars Are Singing" and "Cibola," both relating to the white man's coming into the Indian's world, are again based upon standard historical information—with my contribution being the verbalization of the facts in a language not found in documents or texts.

"Red River" and "Oflaggerty's Child: The Homecoming" are an attempt to summarize into a contemporary personality (myself, my persona) the cultural lessons that the previous eclogues reveal.

Like any writer, I am indebted to certain people for providing inspiration, encouragement, and information. I am especially indebted to my parents, Russell and Edith Weathers, who came to Oklahoma in the early 1920s in the heyday of the Osage renaissance and who recounted to me in my childhood their own experiences and observations of a raw frontier culture with its booming oil industry, its expanding cattle baronies, its bandits and outlaws, and its Indian population. I am indebted, also, to the most famous of the Osage writers, John Joseph Mathews, who does not know me but whom I know through his books *Wah'kon-tah* and *Talking to the Moon*, books that I read as a boy, impressed that someone had made wonderful words about the place where I lived. And I am certainly indebted to the late Lowry C. Wimberly, editor of *Prairie Schooner*, who published the earliest-written of these eclogues—"Hound-Dogs Are Calling" and "Osage August Dances"—when I was still a young man of nineteen and twenty.

THE ECLOGUES

Persimmon Wine

A Chorale for Lonely People in the
Osage Hills

Persimmons fall. And we shall make
persimmon wine. (We shall come
with jars of music into the corners of
our sorrow.)

And winter shall pass. I have seen it fade
along the forsaken creeks of the
Osage, between Okesa and Nelagony,
Gray Horse and Pawhuska. I have seen
it fade through Burbank, Fairfax,
Wizzbang, and Hominy. (Those are
the names of Indian towns.)

Do not be afraid. We shall drink
persimmon wine! Come when the hills
begin to shake with their green and
silent passion. Come when the hills
catch fire with April and the smoke of
the redbud tree lies across the prairie.

Come when the water's green, and
venturing, and first alive.

Pour from the crocks the miracle of wine.
   Who is afraid of what we might have
   been? Or what, so long ago, we
   chanced to be? (But do not die before
   the wine is done. Live for the wine
   that we have made. Live for the
   drinking of the wine that is to come.)

Persimmon wine. And dancing upon the
   waters: Bird Creek and Sand Creek
   and the Caney River. And through the
   sweeping valleys of the sumac and
   the sandstone.

Persimmon wine. And dancing upon the
   face of time: Longhorn cattle far from
   home, the Brahman bulls, the push
   and pull of oil beneath the ground,
   the Katy railcars weeping on the
   wooden trestles, nameless outlaws
   starving in the shadows of the caves.

4

Dancing! Like the driven horses,
scattering and laughing in the fields of
Bigheart, in the pasturelands of Hulah
and Wynona. (Those are the names
of Indian towns.)

We shall make persimmon wine. And
drink the wine. And then lie down.
We shall strip to the wet and loving
roots. Oaks. And cottonwood.
And sassafras. And sycamore. (The
sky is blue with thunder.) Should we
not lie together, the music on our lips?

Sundown over Little Chief. Sweet is the
sound of silence. There is a sudden
flight of mourning doves. The
sun-lashed rain is catching in our hair.
(We shall make persimmon wine.
You come!)

And when the future finds us, let them
say, "They were a magic people in
this ordinary place."

5

Hills That Are Not Easy

1

In the Osage there are the low hills and the high hills.

They are both discernible.

Neither the multitude of trees nor the barrenness of trees distinguishes one hill from another.

I live among the hills in winter, half-winter, and summer. I have seen the trees draw up tightly like dead children to a dead mother.

And in the autumn they are as Attic actors, masked in violent colors.

And in April, they are lonesome ladies.

2

The old men sit at Okesa and speak to the sun:

"Oflaggerty Brown came from Missouri singing on a gray horse and he stopped in the Osage to visit awhile.

"He did not know of the Osage sorrow.

"And after he was in the Osage a passage of time, he got him a job on a big ranch.

"He fell in love with the prairie, but the prairie is pernicious as it is pacific.

"He was a cowpoke on the Osage prairies.

"And Oflaggerty never left.

"Oflaggerty came from Missouri, singing on a gray horse, and he's been a singing no songs ever since. And he's been a singing no songs ever since."

3

You fall in love with the prairie and the prairie women.

They are the beautiful openness of red-buds in the spring, and the beautiful color of sumac in October.

Their laughter is like wind over the sagebrush heart. Their tenderness is a great wide tenderness as sloping hills in slow, majestic rise.

Their coming is a great diurnal surge into the night.

Their coming is a twilight rain over the festered leaves.

Their coming is a shaft of infinite shadow into the bitter room.

They are the light and the dark. They are the sun reflected on the polyangular planes of large rocks, and they are the dark, cool crevices falling between bouldering stones down upon mossy beds.

4

The old men sit at Okesa and speak to the sun:

"Oflaggerty sits toothless now on the fence rail. His days are done. He has grown old with the rest of us, like black oaks gnarled on the hillside.

"See how his fingers reach for the sky?

"He has known the sorrow of prairies and of hills.

"Do you remember how his woman died and they buried her on a hillside looking out over the prairies?

"It is not good for women to die so quickly. Death came cyclonic out of the west edge of the whole world, and tore omnipotently through the field of life.

"And he was left with her child. He and the prairie were left with her child after she was dead."

5

I am Oflaggerty's child.

There are low hills and high hills and I have climbed many hills even when young.

Yet there is one hill that is a high hill and it is a hill that is not easy.

I am sixteen and young, but always my youngness has been on the prairie and in the Osage and the Osage is not young. It is severe with jack oaks that stoop among the sand rocks like old men around a fire.

And the rocks are roughly jutted from the hillside like knots on an old log or like erupted bone through the flesh as I have seen done on dead cattle.

Everything is old in the Osage and there is no room for the new that will not change from new into old.

I have loved the prairie and the prairie hills even as Oflaggerty loved them.

I have ridden wildly on a sable horse through the bluestem grass, darting as an earth-bound eagle through the hills around me.

The prairie has been a mother to me, taking me to her breast of grass and earth, and comforting me. In the rain I have

ridden out to her and I have lain beside
her.

And sometimes on the prairie where the
hills break away and where the earth lies
limitless, curving outward from my eye, I
want to run westward, into the waiting
sky, unbound and new. But I return into
the hollow of the hills that holds me as a
great soft hand.

6

There is one great hill for me. It is there
above them all. I will ride the sable horse
to its high rock summit and lift myself
king on its heaven-toward throne.

Yes. I know. It is a hill that is not easy.
But I am your child, born from you and
the prairie, and with me shall ride the
things of the prairie, the wind, and the
wind-borne brush.

I shall go up in the morning. Through-
out the vicissitude of light and shadow let
me ascend.

11

I am no longer young. Let me lift up into a full height and perceive the full valley.

I will go as you have instructed me. I will go wisely. I shall go singing. Have you been there before me? Do you know how it is?

Shall I see other valleys from the great wide face of the hillside? Will I learn some secret of the prairie that I do not know? Will things change from the vantage-point of there, as you have said they will change? Moonlight from soft chantings to cold, broken chords? Will I know night differently, day transferable? Will I behold the tornado sweeping out from the west horizon?

7

Here then the summit. There then the field.

Around me is the whole world.

There is the sky, blue as a turquoise stone fallen from a great silver ring.

Here is a ring on my finger.

There is the horizon and the other hills, as though a wide belt were scalloped around the earth.

Here is a leathern belt around my waist.

There is the sun and a cloud.

Here is a sunflower by a single white birch.

And here is a marker of five round stones where my mother is buried. I have not been here before. They brought my mother to this high place that she might have the hills and the prairie always about her. I never saw or knew her. All I have known are the things about her and that which was part of her, the earth, the grass, the Osage, and the plains.

There. Far away. Far down. I think I can see Oflaggerty walking slowly, lonely, dried and bent. I think I can see him, toothless, there in the hand of the Osage.

And the sable horse neighs, and stomps, and breaks a piece of silence.

Interlude for Christmas: A Song of the Osage

A tall man lit a cigarette at the foot of the hill. In the moonlight he moved slowly, wearily, his breath blooming white in the cold air in front of him. His eyes ignored the sky above him. He moved slowly, wearily, in his big boots, his head drooping beneath the broad white hat.

I was riding from Pawhuska to Nelagony on a sable horse and I said, "Evening," when I came to the man at the foot of the hill, and he looked up and said, "Evening," letting me know he was an older man than I and letting me know by the face he wore that the Osage was his home. His face was wrinkled where wind had lashed

14

across it, brown where the summer's sun had rained upon it.

"Evening," I said. "Tomorrow's Christmas Day and I'm riding from Pawhuska to Nelagony."

"Tomorrow's Christmas Day," he echoed, "and I'm walking down the road a ways. I'll go along with you until the road turns to go down to the river. Ride slowly, stranger, and we'll go a ways together."

There was a vast prairie of stars above us and cluttered oaks were tense and brittle on the hillsides. Redbuds shivered naked at our side. The hoofbeats of my sable horse fell slowly along the moonlit winding road. The man moved slowly, wearily through the cold night beside me.

"Tomorrow's Christmas Day," he said, "and I'm walking to the graveyard my folks have, there where the road turns to go to the river. There's a graveyard there with four marble stones and a stoneless grave, and a small twisted pine that

15

shudders in the wind. Tomorrow's Christmas Day and I've come down from the ranch house to visit the grave. Ride slowly, stranger, and we'll go a ways together."

It's a narrow road and a winding road that leads from Pawhuska to Nelagony, and on a hillside is a ranch house that looks down over the road, the river, and the graves that lie together around the wind-blown twisted pines.

"I walk down from the ranch house on Christmas Eve. My son is buried here where the road turns. My grandparents, my parents, and my only son are here. All have stones except my child, but he was young, oh far too young, to bear the heavy load of rocks. The earth is heavy enough. He must wait until I lie beside him to hold the granite that will mark his grave. He must wait until I lie beside him and hold the awful weight that a tomb can make."

The night was cold. The road turned.

"Ride slowly, stranger. The night is long. I turn here."

From the large pocket in his wool jacket the man pulled a long string of twisted ribbon, a rope of red and silver shininess, and in the moon it glistened.

"It has been thirty years," he said softly. "He was small then. I often wonder how he lies here now. His mother dreams of him yet—that little child all light and shadow, tears and smiles, but I sometimes see a long, lonely cowhand lying here, a boy turned man, with strong hands and smooth light-muscled legs. I see him sleeping with a calm half-smile upon his face and a red scarf around his neck, a long rope by his side."

The road turned, but I stood still.

"He loved the tinseled ribbon on the Christmas trees. I come on Christmas Eves.

"Oh, someday I will die! And then I'll hold the granite stone for him and strangers passing by will read: Son of the Osage and Child of the hills, Herder of cattle and Roper of steers, Hunter of coyotes and Killer of wolves."

Wind wandered through the gnarled pine and the man slung the ribbon over the scraggly branches. The ribbon burned silverly in the moonlight. The branches swayed. The man turned heavily and sighed "Merry Christmas" into the wind.

It's a narrow road and a winding road that leads from Pawhuska to Nelagony. Redbuds shivered naked by the side.

"Ride slowly, stranger," the man called back to me. And I rode on.

Tse'Cabe

1

Sitting in the bright sun are the old women and on their hand is the black spider. These are the old women of the Osage, and they are high honored, and proudly they turn their hand to the sun and let the sun see their honor.

The black spider is Tse'Cabe and is a great mark, and Tse'Cabe is old in the Osage.

Listen, and I will tell you what these women are thinking. These three women are ancient and are thinking how the Tse'Cabe is a great symbol, and how the Tse'Cabe is tattooed upon them.

Listen, and I will tell you their legend.

2

In the beginning there were the tree peoples walking in the great forests and over the long prairies and around the hills. There were the Children of the Sky and they were called Chest'to. There were the Children of the Earth and they were called Hunkah. There were the Children of the Water and they were called Wah Sha She.

Now each of these peoples was of many clans and each clan took a symbol. Each symbol was for greatness and virtue and for good shooting and swift running. Each clan had a symbol except one of the Hunkah, and the Hunkah clan could find no mark. This clan could not take the bear for they were not strongest. This clan could not take the buffalo for they were not the most numerous. This clan could not take the panther for they were not the stealthiest. This clan could not take the eagle for they were not swiftest. This clan could not take the wolf for they were not most dangerous.

3

"Let us go," said a warrior, "into the forest seeking our symbol. Let us go find a symbol to be our own. Let us seek a fitting token to do us honor and to do our children honor."

The clan of the Hunkah went walking into the deep forest. The clan of the Hunkah went over the soft grass and around the berry bushes seeking a symbol fitting their people. Now it is a great honor to be a symbol and the animals came to the clan in order to be the symbol. But the clan kept walking for they had not yet found a good token.

The coyote came and said, "I will be a good symbol and no clan has chosen me."

But the clan of the Hunkah said, "You are slinking coward and we do not want you." And they walked on.

Wah Pokah, the owl, came and said, "I am a good symbol and no clan has chosen me."

But the clan of the Hunkah said, "You are a foolish bird with a funny face and we do not want you."

4

Now finally when the clansmen were weary and worn from the walking in the forest and when they had found no token and of all the Osage they had no token, Tse'Cabe came and said, "I will be a good symbol and no clan has chosen me."

The clan of Hunkah laughed and said, "You are only a black spider and we do not want you."

But Tse'Cabe said, "I will be a good symbol and bring honor to your clan and to the Osage."

And the warriors said to Tse'Cabe, "What are your virtues?"

Tse'Cabe said, "Wherever I am I build my house. Where I build my house, all things come to it and break their necks therein."

Now the clan of the Hunkah took the black spider as a token and it became a great symbol in the Osage and it became the symbol of home and of women.

5

Sitting in the bright sun are the old women and on their hand is the Tse'Cabe. These are the old women of the Osage and they are high honored, and proudly they turn their hand to the sun and let the sun see their honor.

Listen, and I will tell you how the Tse'Cabe is a great symbol through all the clans and through the Osage, and I will tell you how it is the great token of home and women.

Sitting in the bright sun are the three old women and they are smiling deep inside for they have high honor and have been good women and made good homes. Few women in the Osage have sat in the sun with the black spider upon them. The black spider is Tse'Cabe and is a great mark, and Tse'Cabe is old in the Osage.

Wah-kon-tah-och-kee-ah: He Talked with God

1

Soft lie the tumbleweeds over his grave.

Soft moves the river between the two hills.

And soft moves the wind among the low grasses where the Salt Creek turns to the north and the east.

Long has he lain here and long has he been but dust. And the rusty arrow falls from his head. And I will tell of the Osage prophet whom the Osage call Wah-kon-tah-och-kee-ah. For he was a man who talked with God. And he was a medicine man, friend of the buzzards.

2

Night and the birds come softly home,
to roost in the camp of the medicine man,
to roost in the knotted oak of the Osage
hill. And a buzzard walked to the tepee
fire: Wah-kon-tah-och-kee-ah, listen and
a famine shall fall on the people.

Nor did the buffalo come from the
south and the Osage moaned by the edge
of Salt Creek and the Osage moaned in
Cyclone Hollow. Nor did the buffalo
come from the south and the Osage ate of
the yet green pumpkin, green like the new
grass and small like the walnut. And the
unfit rabbit was sought in the forest and
the despicable hare was brought to the fire.

But a buzzard walked by the tepee
twice: Wah-kon-tah-och-kee-ah, the buffalo come from the south, and the buffalo
gather at Red Rock Creek. And yet an
enemy comes with the bounty and a
danger lurks in the quest of food.

Night and the birds came softly home, and the warriors came to the camp of the prophet, to sleep through the darkness, to seek in the morning the bounteous herd.

Wah-kon-tah-och-kee-ah said: I have talked with the buzzards and there is an enemy come up with the buffalo and if you go hunting, the buzzards have told me, then I shall die.

But the warriors were hungry and eager for food and the children were crying in the arms of their mothers. "You are old and afraid to die." And the warriors taunted and slept for the hunt.

3

Morning came and the birds took wing, and the prophet appeared in a bright red coat, a coat that the Osage got from a white man, and the coat was long and red like the sunrise.

The prophet went with the warriors and hunters till they came to the edge of the Crescent and Wah-kon-tah-och-kee-ah said: The buzzards have told me I shall die, for an enemy lurks with the buffalo herd.

But the warriors pressed on and the hunters pressed on and came to the buffalo on Red Rock Creek. With a cry to the wind and a cry to the earth the warriors plunged into the killing and the fat bulls fell and the choicest cows.

Now I will tell you of the lurking tribe that appeared on the hillside bent on the Osage. And I will tell you the enemy was great with many arrows and many war-riors. And the Osage were forced to take to the creek and many were killed and many were dead. And I will tell you how the red-coated prophet stood on the creek bank and called to the enemy, drawing the arrows away from the Osage. Long did the Osage creep down the river and long did the prophet stand on the bank. But then there was sundown and an arrow came, like the flight of a bird, like the flight of a buzzard, and the arrow came home to the top of his head.

And the Osage took him and he was not dead. "I shall live. The buzzards have told me and I shall live if you will leave me inside a thick thicket. The buzzards will save me in less than five days. But if you should take me, I shall but die."

And the Osage left him inside a high thicket and the buzzards came and circled about him.

4

Wah-kon-tah-och-kee-ah lay like a wounded cardinal. He lay and the buzzards walked around him chanting his cure.

Get you up and be living,
The tarantulae come from the cave

And the moon is a bird on a golden wing.
Get you up and be living,
Eat of the cacti, drink of the dew,
And the river rolls, by day and by night.
The croak of the vulture is heavy with
  wisdom
And our wings crack with lightning
And our breath with thunder.
Get you up and be living.

But when the warriors had come to the camp then they were taunted and the old men said: Where is the prophet?

And the women said: Where is the prophet?

And the warriors said: He is yet living in a high thicket for he has said the buzzards will cure him. But for fear you will think us cowards, we will go bring him back to the camp.

The warriors came back to the riverside thicket, startled the buzzards, lifted him up, carried him home to the camp by the

Salt Creek, and now I will tell you he died
in a fortnight and never was cured.

5

Soft lies the tumbleweed over his
grave. Singing his fame and chanting his
wisdom, the Osage had laid him into the
earth, wearing his red coat, bearing the
arrow that robbed him of living.

Long have the buzzards screamed of
his greatness, long have they come to the
trees by his grave, and yet do they talk
to him, telling the future.

Long has he lain here and long has he
been but dust. And now I have told you
of the Osage prophet, Wah-kon-tah-och-
kee-ah. For he was a man who talked
with God. And he was a medicine man,
friend of the birds.

The Rite of the Chiefs

1

The sun sets. Great heaps of cloud are gathered in the sky like golden wigwams on a blue prairie. And the night curls up from the east like a dark smoke.

In the orange cups of the trumpet vine the dew gathers and soon will fall like a cascade of silver over the sands and the rocks of the Osage hill. Even now the sound of the locust falls over the edge of dusk.

The sun sets like a crimson bird soaring to rest into the tree-top of another world.

On this bluff we sit, you and I, and I think that we are like two crows, perched on the dark limb of the earth, gazing into a valley of legends. Do you remember the tale of our people? Do you remember the rite of the chiefs? In the evening I think of the legends of the Osage, when the sun goes down and these shadows fall over us.

2

There was a time when our fathers were like mist in the sky, like that mist which sleeps at the curve of the river and steals away at dawn like a pale fox from the fields.

And our fathers were like the fog that crumbles over the hillside in formless whispers, like the fog that a silver spider spins into a wide, shimmering web.

Our fathers were like the smoke which floats from the tepee on an autumn day and the children ask, "Where does the smoke go?" for it becomes pale and invisible as it brushes against the autumn sky.

Thus it was the leader of our race said, "Lo, younger brother, we are like mist in the sky and our voices float strangely like soft smoke, hither and yon, nor do we have bodies that we may walk over the prairie or that we may pick the persimmon from the winter tree. Lo, younger brother, let our people gather together as one cloud or as many leaves on one twig or as many stars in a sky and let us search for hands and legs, and not only hands and legs, but even ears and eyes."

Now, as when winter comes and the buffalo surge southward toward the greener grasses, so our fathers surged forward into the heavens until at last they came to the North Star and they said, "Lo, Grandfather, we are without bodies."

And the North Star answered, "Can I give you bodies? I am not the only mysterious one. Search even farther."

Our fathers moaned like a lost north wind and moaned through the universe until they came to the Morning Star. "Lo, Grandmother," our fathers said, "we are without bodies."

But the Morning Star replied, "Can I give you bodies? I am not the only mysterious one. Search even farther."

And our fathers, like a flight of angry bees, flew to the Three Deer and the Small Star, to the Sun, and the Moon, but all of them answered: "Can I give you bodies? You are to search a little while longer."

And so it was our fathers came to rest on the top of a red-oak tree, came to rest like rain on the branches or snow on the leaves. And as a young squaw sings in the night to the young papoose, so did the murmur of our fathers sound among the branches and the leaves of the red-oak tree.

3

Now do you remember there was a Red-Bird in the top of the tree, nesting there as an apple grows reddest high on the apple tree? Like a wild rose midst a bush of green leaves and thorns, the Red-Bird nested midst the thick leaves of the oak tree. "Lo, brethren," our fathers sighed, like a mournful spring breeze among the tall grasses, "we are without bodies even though we have searched as far as the stars."

But the Red-Bird said, "I can cause you to have human bodies from my own.

" My left wing shall be a left arm for the children and my right wing a right arm.

" My head shall be their head and my mouth their mouth.

" My forehead shall be their forehead and my neck their neck.

" My throat shall be their throat and my chest their chest.

" My bowels shall be their bowels and my thighs their thighs.

" My knees shall be their knees and my calves their calves.

" My heels shall be their heels and my

36

toes their toes, and even my claws shall
become their toenails and you shall
continue to exist unharmed. Your children shall live as human beings and I shall
bestow the speech of children upon your
children and the Osage people shall be
forever."

4

Now as when spring comes and a tree
blooms, and the new leaves unfold,
silently and amazingly, so our fathers
unfolded out of the mist onto the branches of the red-oak tree. As when at
twilight the leaves are yet unopened but
at dawn are full on the twigs, so our
fathers were one moment nothing but
like air, and the next moment were tall
men with long arms and handsome legs.
As when in the autumn the leaves come,
one by one, to earth, so now our fathers
came one by one to earth at last.

Lo, are the footprints marked over the prairie? Lo, in many paths out from the campfire.

Lo, are the fruits brought down from the tree? The frosted persimmon is plucked from the winter tree and brought to the wigwam for the winter's night.

Thus it was the Osage people came from the sky to the land, came as cousins to the Red-Bird, came as builders of a great nation.

5

The sun sets. Great heaps of cloud are gathered in the sky like gray wigwams on a sable prairie. Night whimpers on the edge of the world like a coal-black hound at the edge of the campsite.

Did you see how the sun set like a red-bird, circling low and lower? Did it stir some old feeling within you? Do you ever see a cardinal in the forest and think,

"There goes my cousin. From his flesh
my people came"?

On this bluff we sit, you and I, and I
am thinking, "Lo, the red blood flows
within my veins."

But darkness falls. The locust calls.
And we must go.

Pah-se-to-pah:
Hunter of the Osage

1

He was a huntsman of the Osage hills, riding over the bluestem grass, among the knotted blackjack trees.

He was a great rider on a great horse and in the Indian parades along Ki-he-kah Street he would wear his great headdress of many eagle feathers. He was the leader of many parades in Pawhuska, for he was a huntsman and a great Osage. Now there are parades in the Osage without him, and he no longer rides among the rolling hills along Bird Creek and Sand Creek.

He is a dead Indian gone hunting in grassier fields and over broader hills. He is gone to a lovelier Osage where even darker eagles fly and clearer rivers flow.

2

I will tell you what I have heard of Pah-se-to-pah, hunter of the Osage. I, myself, have seen him leading the Indians in from Indian camp for the great parades.

I will tell you how he was deaf and dumb and spoke to us all in his quick signs and strange signs, his brown fingers reciting the finger-language of his people.

I will tell you how he was a child in the Osage, playing with his brothers and sister, St. John and Shapahnashe and Dora.

And I will tell you how he would race over the country on a prairie horse. And I will tell you how one day in a long race with other Indian boys his wild horse rolled over the embankment. And I will tell you how after that he never heard or spoke again.

3

Pah-se-to-pah was twelve years old and learned a proud pantomime with his eager face and his eager hands.

The Osages had migrated from Neosho into the Osage country and in the Osage there were wild deer and turkey. Early in the saddle, with bow and arrow and for him a silent rifle, Pah-se-to-pah shot many birds and beasts and collected his eagle feathers.

Hunter of the Osage he was called and after each hunting he gathered white feathers and soon there were many. And when he was a full warrior and a great teller of tales and recaller of legends, he made him a headdress of seventy-four feathers and it hung high on his head down by his back and swept on the ground.

4

Pah-se-to-pah was a resplendent Osage and he would wear the great headdress even in the great parades he led in Washington when he went for his people to the site of a nation.

He was known all over for his hand-words and his bright Osage eyes, and he was a hunter all his life.

I will tell you how I saw him last, along with his people at a famous dance. Pah-se-to-pah was a hunter and a dancer. He was a big and good dancer. And I will tell you how he could not hear the drum-beats, steadily sounding, but never lost step with any of the others. I will tell you how he kept good time dancing around in the great circle of Osage dancers, keeping good time by watching the drummers and the drumkeepers, steadily and constantly, lifting the drumbeats.

5

He was a huntsman of the Osage hills, riding over the bluestem grass, among the knotted blackjack trees. He was a greater rider on a greater horse than many others, and he had family and children.

Now he is no longer a wearer of white eagle feathers nor a hunter among the low hills of the Osage or along the warm and sandy creeks of the Osage.

He is a dead Indian gone to a lovelier Osage where even darker crows call lonely in the twilight and even brighter sumacs burn in autumn.

Hound-Dogs Are Calling

The hound-dogs are calling at the moon.

I am a wanderer among the blackjacks and watcher of the campfires. And I listen to the legends told in the twilight and the sunset.

I listen to them talk of John Stink and the ghost of him, and I walk by the wig-wam and the cabin on the hill.

I walk the road of Skyline Drive and stir the dust in the evening air, and I remember their words:

"John Stink was always very old."

"He wore a scarf about his head; tied it under his neck like a woman would."

"He smoked black cigars and blew smoke in soft strange circles."

"John Stink was always very old."

There was a day they speak of when the town of Pawhuska was still alive and the oil wells were still drinking up the Osage wealth and the pioneer blood was vital and vigorous.

It was a day when there was color on the streets and the Osages were many on Ki-he-kah, and their Cadillacs circled the Triangle Building and drove up Grand View to the agency.

He came down from his wigwam on Sky-line Drive and with him came his dogs, hound-dogs and common dogs, five in all.

He walked in from the west, over Bird Creek, into Main Street, for it was Saturday. Saturday was a day for coming to town and there was much color.

John Stink was old even then, older than years had numbered, and old in the deep brown wrinkles of his face. He shuffled along the streets and looked with his dark solemn eyes at the windows of the stores—looked with ancestors in his

46

blood who had not known the oil boom or the riggings of the white men or the new things of a new world.

And his dogs scurried close to him and whimpered with being away from the still country.

It was a day of growth in Pawhuska and there were laws that were pertinent to growth; among the frameworks of boom-town banks and barrooms and pool halls there were little laws that mean nothing to anyone.

The bullets came sharply in the day-light because he did not understand; the chanting, softly shrill Osage tongue could not say, nor the ancient Osage mind understand.

The sheriff knew John Stink and meant no harm, but Indians were Indians and dogs were dogs and there was no license and there was a law.

John Stink shuffled back to Skyline Drive, as old as ever, and he sat that night in the wigwam, dogless, and he never came to town again.

"He never would ride in an automobile. Once we stopped on the road in front of the wigwam and he came to the fence and stared at us."

"He would never live in the fine log house the agency built for him; he slept and stayed in the wigwam even in the winter days."

"He gave a party once for the children of Indian Camp and gave them black cigars; he was not unkind."

"John Stink was always very old."

There are many explanations. One has it that he went off with smallpox and stayed away hidden in his sickness and returned well. Or that he slept and was not dead.

But I hear it from the old squaws and the old braves as they surround the campfire that he was dead and come to life again.

He, who was always old, lay in the sun on the rocks by the wigwam and the women found him and found him dead.

He, who was always old, lay in the sun on the rocks by the wigwam and the women found him and found him dead and laid rocks upon him because of his deadness.

And the night came. Lonely Osage night, and there was sleep among the people.

And they who had found him and buried him kept a chanting watch in his wigwam as it was good to do. He, who was always old, was now gone on his long journey. And they kept a chanting watch.

But near the dawn of the day there was heard the rolling of stones and the sound of walking on the grass, and the dead one stood in the wigwam and they who had

49

found him and buried him cried out in their tongue, "It is the ghost of him!"

And the ghost of him haunted the hill for many years, day and night, and the legend grew until many people knew of John Stink and his dying and his coming back again.

I have seen him sitting on the rocks outside the wigwam and the smoke was climbing from the tepee's opening. As the smoke arose, he blew from a black cigar soft smoke rings into the air and held a rock in his old brown hand and put it down again.

Even ghosts die and one day he was ill and they took him into the fine log cabin and he died there. And he did not stir up the stones again.

I am a wanderer among the blackjacks and redbuds and I am a watcher of the campfires, and I listen to the legends told in the twilight and sunset, told to the rhythm of oil wells throbbing.

And I walk the road of Skyline Drive and see the cabin and the wigwam.

I walk where he walked, and at the opening of the tepee I stop, for inside I think I see the shadow of the ghost of him, and I think I hear the ghost-like, spirit-like call of hound-dogs to the moon.

Osage August Dances

Let me undress from the white world
And step from the new closet
Into the old wideness. I hear the drums
Softly and neatly, beckoning me
Into the world of bright color.
A feather for the deep lake running
    within me.
And a feather for the sky and earth and
    the soft smoke, ascending.
And a feather for the supple skin over the
    strong limbs in wigwam and body.
And jingling bells in far-away calling.
(A costume for my soul.)
Let my muscles ripple through my thighs
    and lead me strongly
Through the patterns of my people and
    my fathers.

2

I hear the drums, neatly besieging
The mind, indigenous,
And the long arm reaches
Beyond our conceptions.
I will take feathers and walk toward the
    gathering
Singing and chanting in drum-beating
    rhythm.
Sun will shine on me and glisten my color
And I will reflect in bronze adoration
The things of the hillside and things of
    the valley
And eagles flying upon the blue sky.

I will come freely into the rainbow
Chanting the spectrum, singing the
    sunlight.
Leaving the closet of faded wild-roses.
Walking in silence upon the dry grasses.

And here are the others, the warriors, the
    people,

Assembled, addressing, in blankets of
   blackness
And eyelids of oldness. Here are the
   drummers
Keeping the edges beaten and rounded
Into the centuries, trailing behind us.

3

All through my body the warm blood is
   singing
And my feet in soft leather are nervous
   and moving.
Fathers and sons are naked and native.
Loins are tightened like clustered
   persimmons
Frosted in winter with strength and
   fertility.
And warrior faces are painted in scarlet
Bled from the berries on low bushes
   growing.
(Cover our bodies in soft woven clothing
And dance with the bells tinkling
   beside us

And feathers are growing up over our
    faces
And fur-tails are dangling on wrists and
    on ankles.)

The drummers are starting the routinous
    beat.
Lift up our memory, raise up our feet
And into the dust and over the clay
And through the thickness of August's
    hot day
Repeat the soft stomping that echoes
    with age.

4

Let us rotate, circular
About the drums, sacred.
Fathers and sons, bending
Earthward and skyward.

Quickly our glances
Upward and downward,

Swiftly our movements
Sharply and smoothly.

We are the panther,
The eagle, flying,
We are the buffalo,
The turkey and deer.

Warriors in strenuous
Gesticulation,
Vivid communion
With vigorous nature.

Louder the drumbeat,
Higher the calling,
Ripple the shrill tongue
Warbled and wavered.

And the dark old ones,
In old animation,
Long hair in dark braids
And old faces darkened.

Let them do tail dances
Slowly toward center.
Then the quick stopping,
And then the quick silence.

5

Inward the warriors,
Outward the women,
Men in gay feathers,
Women in blankets.

Warriors in fervor,
Women in calmness,
All in one rhythm,
All in one dancing.

Nearest the drumbeat
The loud-shouting warriors.
Outward toward nature
The all-silent maidens.

Old squaw and papoose,
The tan-faded feather.

In small step and low step
Marking the dust.

And maidens in doeskin,
Sun-white and moon-white.
Dancing near warriors,
Brave and virgin.

6

Where in the dances are old faces hidden?
John Stink and Bacon Rind and Osage
    chieftains?
Where is Pa-se-to-pah and old Susie
    Blackhawk?
Where is Pawhuska of many years back?
Are they the strange whispers blowing
    among us?
Are they the drum-echoes silent upon us?

Where have our fathers gone dancing
    this summer,
In fields of great hunting and lodges of
    sweetness?

Do they remember their families and
    children
Far in the distance beside the great river,
Then the great prairie, then the low hills?

Our fathers, our chieftains are wakened
    from sleeping,
Moved from their hunting, stirred from
    their peace.
The drummers are beating songs for the
    ancients,
Songs for the living. We are the dancers,
The living, the ancient, the fathers and
    sons.

7

August has fallen,
Dances are given,
Tribes are assembled
Of Osage and Ponca.

Feasts are partaken
Of squaw-bread and jerked meat.

Children are playing
With spotted, lean dogs.

Dry leaves are scattered
Under the oak trees,
Winds from the south sun
Rustle and crush them.

How are the warriors
And how are the wars?
Dance for the dead ones
Silent and gone.

Walk in the sunlight,
Dance in its brightness.
Move in the nighttime,
Move in its shadow.

Dance in the moon, three-quarter risen,
Ing-thus-ka dances,
Leading young warriors
Into the patterns.

8

And after the dances, lengthy and stirring,
After the beaters of drums, and
　　drum-keepers
Have spoken in silence and not in their
　　rhythms,
We shall take feathers down from our hair.

Undo our trappings,
Scented with dancing,
We must go back
Into the closet.

Forsake what is native,
The past is our dream.
A pale shadow haunts us
And falls in our eyes.

Turn to the city
Of colorless towers.
The world is too small
And time must go on.

Death of a Choctaw

1

Now there is this story about the Choctaws which are a good people. I will tell
you this story about the Choctaws, who
have a council house at Tuskahoma, and
you will remember what I have said.

I will not tell you about the Choctaws
when they were in Mississippi and how
they built churches and schools. I will not
tell you of Pushmataha who spoke for his
people at Doak's Stand with Andrew
Jackson. I will not tell you how the
Choctaws were at Dancing Rabbit Creek
and began the great move, nor will I tell
you how the Choctaws searched to find
rich land for farming, deep streams for
fishing, thick forests for hunting, and
grassed prairies for riding.

Only I will tell you that the Choctaws

were in Oklahoma and found deer and
bear and wild turkey and buffalo.

2

The Choctaws have no jails for they
are an honest people and one of them
who is a wrongdoer returns for his
punishment for he is a good warrior.
One who is a good warrior comes on the
certain day to pay his fine, to take his
lashes, to be hanged, or to be shot.

There is this legend of great honor
among the Indians, and it is of great
bravery, also. It is a Choctaw youth who
was to die for his killing, for even in his
youngness he had done wrong and had
killed a warrior.

Who is that coming in to town? That
is the one to die. He will die for he is a
killer.

What does he come for? He comes to
choose his coffin and his dressing. He will

be buried like a white man with a coffin
and with clothes.

The Choctaws have no jail and the
wrongdoers come to town to choose their
coffins and their clothes.

3

What day is this? This is the day of
dying.

Who is that coming in to town? That
is the one to die. He is coming with his
family and they walk in a deep silence.

What do they come for? To bury his
body.

Who is that woman? She is his mother
and she is combing his hair before he is
dead.

What is he doing? He is touching his
family and saying farewell, for this is his
last goodbye.

Where is he going? He walks to the
great tree where others have died, and he

turns to the people, and makes his breast naked.

Who is to kill him? He has chosen a friend with whom he was young. His good friend has a good gun and will shoot straight and with good aim.

Now he is dead.

4

The Choctaws are a good people and swift in their justice. There are no jails for warriors have honor.

There is no flight among their brave people. He who is to die comes with his mother and she will comb his hair and the law will be done.

And they will bury him in his coffin and in his clothes. He is a good warrior who does not flee, but comes to the great tree, unfettered and unforced, and proudly pays the debt for his crime.

I have told you this tale of the Choctaws, and you will remember.

Peyote

1

Here, by the old tree, share the shadow of the afternoon with me, and we shall remember the legends and I shall tell you of the spirit which has come to the Delaware.

I am an old man, with twilight on my face, but there is still the light of the late sun in my eyes and my thoughts are sharp as the sandstone rock which stands sharply on the west side of the hill.

And my heart still beats as the tom-tom beats, and I have seen many oak leaves bloom and fall, and now I will tell you of a new religion and a new cause which makes me happy even when I hear the lone coyote call or see some star, late in the dark night, break from the sky and fall.

2

Now I will tell you how it all began back even before I was a papoose, but all this I have heard from my mothers and my fathers. These years ago the Comanche people went all together into the direction that the loud birds fly when the winters are coming, and in the nighttime, the Comanche would steal upon the strange Indians who live nearer the sun, and there was war among them called the Mexicans and them called the Comanche, and this is how it was.

Now as a squaw chases a hare from the little garden along the creek bank, so did the wild, dark Indians pursue the Comanche, and many were the war cries and the gay feathers flying, but the Comanche were faster and they fled over the prairie.

Now there was an old squaw who was good for her cooking, but now she was sick and old and it was time for her dying, and she said to them, "Leave me near a big rock or beneath a big tree that the wind may not beat against me nor the sun strike me, for I can go no farther and it is time for me to lie and look at the sky forever."

The Comanche are not cruel as some people are, leaving their old women out for the snakes to crawl over and coyote to find, but they put her by a great rock and beneath a thick tree, and they left her with food and good water. And they left her with a little boy who would be with her, even until she died. Now the Comanche fled onward, on to the west, and the sun made a golden road down which they galloped, and when they had outrun the enemy, the Comanche would return for the Indian boy and for the old woman, whether her eyes were open or closed.

3

Now when the night came as dark as the wings of a hilltop crow, the little

68

child sat shivering even as the winds moved on the twisted tree limbs, and he was thinking of his people who had gone with the sun, and he saw the old woman was either dead or sleeping, and when the moon crawled like a golden spider up the black wall of the sky, the child could see the horse tracks still thick in the dust, and he began to follow them, and he ran faster and faster until he could run no more and as a small star slides beneath a cloud, the child fell beneath a grove of trees and then he went to sleep.

Yet as a mother stirs when her baby is taken from her, so did the old squaw wake in the middle of night and reach to feel the soft child beside her, but there was nothing there but the dark earth itself, and she knew the child had gone for his people. "Child!" she called in her old voice. "Where are you? Our people have gone with the sun and you cannot find them. You shall be lost and the wild beasts will find you." And the old woman began to crawl in order to find the child, and she pulled herself along the earth after him, saying many prayers to the creator of things, but soon she could move no farther and a great sleep befell her.

4

Now, listen. The desert is a great place where the wind blows and there is a mixture of sound and silence, of shadow and light, and now the desert was silver and black, and the old squaw lay like another rock. (Have you not heard some lonely night the fall of pine needles by the edge of your wigwam?) Now, listen. The old squaw was sick and deaf to all soundings, nor did she hear the soft tread of delicate moccasins come over the desert in silver and black. But the moon saw him coming and the stars saw him coming, and he stood beside her, and like a great chief, even a Comanche, he said to her, softly, in her own language, "Lo, now, woman. I have been watching you come crawling like an old reptile over the desert, and even as a rattlesnake looks for a rabbit, so you come crawling over the prairie after the child. But the child is safe like a star in a cloud, and tomorrow when the sun has arisen, the child shall come to his people. But, lo, now, woman, if I do not help you, you shall wither and die like a leaf that is broken from the life-giving tree. Woman, behold me and see me, and know I have been here, but I shall soon vanish into a flower. Reach out for me, and make me your food, and I shall save you, for I shall be a great comfort to you and your people. A great spirit and a great creator of all things shall sing to you songs, and I am a new spirit for you and your people."

Lo, now, listen. Here was a great chief

in gallant regalia and as at the dusk the
white mist is settling, so now he began
lowering into the ground and soon
he was vanished and soon he was
gone.

But her old dark hand reached out, and
lo, now, listen. A cactus bloomed where
his feet had been standing and the cactus'
flower was a pale, glowing light, and she
began to eat and she felt her soul waken-
ing. And as the stars appear suddenly on
a summer's night and as a moon bursts
from a mountain of thick white cloud, so
did her soul awaken and she was on her
knees and great songs came pouring from
her old, drying throat, and she lifted her
hands and felt the rejoicing. And the
desert was bright and full of a beauty and
the old squaw sang and danced round the
cactus and lo, now, listen, but the flower
sprang upward and there was the chieftain and the moon turned, in a thrilling
rotation, and the wind blew in thunder-

ous ovation, and the chieftain was mighty, and now he was glorious.

"Lo, now, woman. I am Peyote."

5

Here, by the old tree, share the shadows of the afternoon with me, and we shall remember the legends, and I shall tell you of the new spirit which came to the Delaware and to the Comanche and other good Indians all over the prairie.

It is said the old woman came back to her people and made for Peyote a place of worship. From the earth she created a half-moon altar, and behind it built a good burning fire. And she selected good wood and called it especial. And the old woman came back with four songs for singing, and now you have heard them, one at the opening of the Peyote meeting, and one for the water-call when night is half over, and one for the water-call when day is beginning, and one when the meeting for Peyote is over.

Now Peyote is a good spirit sent by the creator, and Peyote gives me a clear mind like a rock on a hillside, and I am kind to my people. When I am ill, Peyote has helped me. And all my life I have walked with Peyote, over the prairie, and he has given me wonderful visions, even of the creator of things. I go to the meeting and I kindle the fire, and I take Peyote into me, and lo, now, listen, he leads me from darkness, and as an eagle soars high over the hilltop, so I soar high over my world. And my head is clear, as in the spring I empty my moccasins of the long winter's ashes.

Now Peyote is good and he is waiting for me. I am an old man with twilight on my face and soon there will be a half-moon in my eyes. I shall become the earth and from my flesh Peyote will grow. Lo, now, listen. I shall be gone to goodness and my soul shall fly like some swift eagle. And Peyote will lead me up over the moon, and there will be singing like wind through the stars. And there shall be singing like wind through the stars and I shall be gone with Peyote.

Last Chief of the Comanches

1

There in the sunlight is his monument, thrust above him toward the prairie sky, and the sky is like a great blue hand, covering him, for he is dead.

He is dead and written above him are these words: Resting here until day breaks and shadows fall and darkness disappears is Quanah Parker, Last Chief of the Comanches.

And beyond the monument is his story. He is buried in a full war dress with granite over him, but beyond him is his story which is spoken among the Quahada and the Comanche.

The old warriors of the Quahada and the Comanche tell their children of the great days when Chief Quanah Parker rode in full war dress upon a white horse.

2

In the many years past the Quahada were a hostile people and were raiders along the borders of Texas. They were led by their Chief Nokoni and they fought valiantly against the encroachments.

Even when the Kiowa and the Cheyennes were at peace, and even when Geronimo was dead and the Apaches stilled, the Quahada were at war and their chief was Nokoni.

In the gray light of a morning in 1836, the Quahada attacked a fort and it was called Parker's Fort and with them came prisoners.

The Quahada took with them two children of the white people and one was a girl and she was called Cynthia Parker.

Cynthia Parker was carried from the fort when she was a child and she grew up to be a woman among the Quahada and she was to marry the Chief Nokoni.

The old warriors tell their children that she became the wife of Nokoni, and she bore a son who was to be called Quanah Parker.

3

Now there was war between the Quahada and the Texas settlers even when the Kiowa and the Cheyennes and Apaches were still, and one night the Rangers invaded the Comanche camp and Nokoni was killed.

Nokoni was killed and he was a great chief to die, but the Rangers were to take some women and children from the Quahada to live with them in their forts.

And as they were looking for the Indian women who were hiding in the camp, they heard a white woman crying and she was mourning, and she was saying, "Me Cynthie, me Cynthie."

The old warriors tell their children how she wished to stay and be with the Quahada and how she wished to bury her husband, but how the Rangers took her back to the white people in Texas.

Now I, who am telling this story, will tell you how sad things happened to Cynthia Parker as though a great crow flew in front of the sun, and I will tell you now how she mourned for Nokoni and she did not bury him, how she mourned for her child who was called Quanah Parker and who was yet with the Quahada, and how she mourned for her daughter-child who bloomed from her and soon died. Like a great crow in the face of the sun, sadness fell upon her and Cynthia Parker mourned and she died, too.

4

Who is the chief now of the Quahada? It is Quanah for he is grown and he remembers his mother, and his father Nokoni is dead.

How does he govern? He is a great leader, but he is a somber, remembering chief who is eager to punish the white peoples because of his father and because of his mother.

Who is this now speaking to him? This is Kicking Bird, an old chief of the Kiowa, asking the Quahada to be peaceful and to bring peace to the plains.

Does Quanah Parker do this? Chief Quanah will not be peaceful for he cannot forget his parents and he roams the prairies seeking the settlers and the buffalo hunters.

How is there peace now? There is peace now, for in 1874 the white peoples defeated the Comanche tribes at the battle of the Adobe Walls, and Quanah Parker was not hostile any longer.

Quanah Parker went to Fort Sill and made a great peace with Colonel McKenzie and the Quahada were the last of the Plains Indians to surrender.

5

I, who am telling this story, will tell you now how Cynthia Parker came home to the Quahada in 1910, to sleep at the Mission of the Post Oak and to bear above her a granite stone.

I will tell you how Quanah Parker gave a great feast for his people and for his mother, who was buried again on one December day.

I will tell you how he spoke in his own tongue of his love for his mother and of her love for the Comanches. In his own tongue he spoke to the Comanches of peaceful ways and of home and of farming. He spoke to the Comanches of the Indian God and the White God which were the same god.

6

There in the sunlight is his monument, thrust above him toward the prairie sky, and the sky is like a great blue hand, covering him, for he is dead.

After his mother came home again to Indiahoma, Quanah Parker died and many thousands of people came to give tribute to him and to be with him in his burial.

He is dead, and lies in his great war dress, and he lies at the side of his mother.

He is dead, and over him on the granite stone are these words: Resting here until day breaks and shadows fall and darkness disappears is Quanah Parker, Last Chief of the Comanches.

The Old Guitars
Are Singing

1

The old guitars are singing on the edge of Texas.

The old, brown hands are picking and playing, throwing gay songs over the Red River.

Roll on, Red River, and I will tell you by the campfire of the march of Gutierrez.

There is the memory of the prairie wind in me, and the remembrance of southern stars.

2

We called him Magee that August day and let him lead us.

One hundred fifty-eight of us followed him that August day across the border and it did not really matter if he were Mexican or American. We were on our way to victory over the Spanish generals and the Spanish king.

On to Nacogdoches was our cry on swift and sturdy horses.

On with Gutierrez was our slogan under the burning Texas sun, over the great wide land.

And I rode there, drunk with being Yankee, fresh from an eastern youth, and I rode there with Gutierrez, spilling independence as I went.

Texas opened up that August day and stretched like a lazy soldier in the sun, washing his face in the deep gulf water.

And the Spanish soldiers went far away to wash their faces in deep gulf water and we laughed at Nacogdoches for it was deserted.

"Freedom for Mexico!" he cried at

84

Nacogdoches and five hundred people joined us.

(Strike a chord for freedom that I may remember.)

We Americans went for freedom and the Mexicans for Gutierrez and we went five hundred strong through Texas.

3

After Nacogdoches there was battle at La Bohia and I counted Spanish soldiers in the Texas sun.

I saw the Spanish generals stand proudly on the distant hills and turn away defeated.

On with Gutierrez was our cry and I was yelling "Yankee," and we came to the cottonwoods at San Antonio.

"Bexar," said the Indians and we camped among the missions and I slept among the tolling bells outside the city.

Among the missions Gutierrez led us
and we heard him murmur, "Salcedo!"
who was a Spanish general.

General Salcedo and General Magee
had seen old times together and General
Magee meant blood to flow here at the
gates of Bexar.

"For freedom!" Gutierrez had told us,
so we fought and won and split the city
of cottonwoods through to its Spanish
heart and we marched like Spanish generals through the streets.

(Strike a chord for freedom that I may
remember.)

San Antonio fell for freedom and the
Mexicans wept for freedom and we
Yankees laughed for Yankee ways here in
the heart of Texas.

But the Spaniards moaned for murder
when Salcedo died.

I remember the silver trappings and
the silver sword and how Gutierrez had
stolen them when Salcedo died.

And Salcedo had been murdered by our good man Magee and we Yankees all stopped laughing and rode away.

(Strike a chord for freedom that I may remember.)

I hear he reached Natchitoches late one night with only a handful of straggling followers. After we had left him the cry for freedom was still.

4

We Yankees rode away and I rode away from Texas and I didn't come back for many years.

But Texas kept fighting and yelling and cussing and growing and then came the great names like Long and Austin and Travis and Houston and freedom rang again without me over the southern plains.

There was no blood on my hands, but I washed them off in the river.

And Gutierrez went to Natchitoches carrying a silver sword and I rode north out of Texas.

Now I am old and things are all different. We were not so gallant at San Antonio as to be written down. It took the Alamo.

But we were a fighting lot under old Magee.

Now the old guitars are singing on the edge of Texas.

Old brown hands are plucking and playing, throwing gay songs over the Red River.

Roll on, Red River, and let me lie, not too far from the flickering light, and under a Texas sky.

Cibola

1

I am the city of Cibola.

My towers burn in the sun. I am gold even to the roofs of my structures and to the pavements of my thoroughfares.

I am a fabulous legend whispered through the centuries. Lone travelers have come from strange journeys, and they have spoken mysteriously of seeing my walls far in the distance.

My towers are blinding in the noon and haunting in the midnight. I am the ancient remnant of some lost world, some vague culture, and some forgotten people.

Many have sought me, but none has found me. I am still here. Many have come over the deserts and over the blue mountains, but I elude them.

2

I saw him coming far across the fields, and he was coming gallantly. Bold and new he came in silver and bronze, as brilliant as any had ever come up from Mexico toward me. And around him were the soldiers of his army and the people of his conquering, and I heard in their murmuring his name, and his name was Coronado.

He rode proudly on a fine horse, and to the east was the sun breaking over the horizon, hanging in the sky like a bright Spanish copper. Over each river and past each mountain he looked for me, but I was not there for I would move on as the day progressed.

I saw him come, and as he came the verdant land changed, and it changed to a desert with sagebrush and cactus and there was no living thing.

At night in his sleep, Coronado dreamed

of me, and he visioned his riding upon my cobblestones in the brilliance of some future day and crying upward past my towers, "I am the Conquistador! Long live the king!"

3

The Indian Turk told them of my legend and spoke of my being farther north, and the weary group set out again in search of me. I was their dream and their hope for I was and am of great goldness and beauty and treasure.

On and on they came, northward, and even I grew weary with their coming. Their silver and bronze had lost its glitter, and the proud horses were thin and becoming weak.

Coronado dreamed fitfully now, and he did not guess I was so near as just another dream away.

I was not surprised when he took his strong Spanish hands in a mood of temper and squeezed the neck of the Indian guide until the eyes leaped out in horror. As he died, the Indian gasped my name, "Cibola!"

Coronado breathed heavily and cried, "Cibola! Where are you!"

And I laughed on the wind and hid in the shadow of the mountain that was by his right hand.

4

I am the city of Cibola, and few have come toward me after him.

If he had come around the last hill and over the last river and looked far in the distance he might have seen my lustrous dimensions.

Coronado turned south, leaving the bones of the Indian Turk to bleach in the sun, for the Indian had promised me but had not delivered me.

Coronado turned south, and I do not know if he ever roamed again.

I hear he died.

But even now, four centuries have passed. The legend of me is gone with the ashes of the old dreamers and the old travelers. Some have sought me even yet, out alone in the wide, untreed prairies or on some extending summit.

Even now, four centuries have passed, and in the night his spirit seeks me. At the portals of my outer walls the spectre of Coronado comes, and he pounds heavily and hysterically, and he calls, "Cibola!"

I am the city of Cibola.

My towers burn in the sun. I am gold even to the roofs of my structures and to the pavements of my thoroughfares.

I lean near him and whisper to him and show him the way across the hills and river. *That is the way*, I say, and he turns eagerly, and I lead him.

The bronze trappings and the silver armour are rusted and decayed.

93

The proud white horse is a weird and galloping phantom.

I laugh. I am Cibola. I lead him up over the blue mountains and over the wide rivers. The Conquistador! I lead him into his own oblivion that is eternal want and some unending search.

Red River

Let us cross the river and rest under the shade of the trees. General Stonewall Jackson. The Civil War. He spoke those words before he died, looking I suppose across some river back east in Virginia or South Carolina or wherever it was his final battle had managed to bring him. Let us cross the river and rest. . . . Not relevant at all, really, to the river that flows between Oklahoma and Texas, stretching out sad and lonesome in the Southwestern sun. Not relevant. But I think of his words, nevertheless, when I cross Red River. I make his words the slogan of my crossing and my journey.

Five years ago I crossed Red River in a 1962 Chevrolet Impala, gunning down Highway 75 that takes you from Durant to Denison. It was a beautiful day. About nine o'clock in the morning. Spring was in the air. May 17. And right there on the bridge I ran into a swarm of yellow butterflies. A thousand pieces of yellow tissue paper blown by the wind. They rose up before me and scattered into the sky. Yellow everywhere. I slowed way down and drove with great and deliberate beauty through their delicate presence. Careful, careful.

When I got to Denison I stopped at the Mobil gas station and had a Dr. Pepper. Five gallons of premium. No oil needed. The day was getting warm and the Dr. Pepper was sweet and cold. I was a beautiful person, traveling with music in my head. I was a beautiful person, traveling with secrets in my blood.

One yellow butterfly was crushed on the grill at the front of the car. I asked the filling station attendant if he couldn't clean it off. He did.

Long before I ever crossed Red River I had heard its name. My father used to sing a song about it. My father would sing in the dark, after I'd gone to bed. I was six or seven then, and my father would sit in the wicker rocking chair beside my bed and in the darkness he'd sing until I went to sleep. He sang a song about "Springtime in the Rockies" and another song about "Red River Valley." I don't remember the words at all, but I remember the songs were sad and lonesome.

My father was a short, stocky man. A carpenter. He never sang any other time in his life. Only for me. In the darkness.

Red River Valley. Something about time past and love that was lost. All I really remember is the name. The name of the place. And the sounds of my father's voice, a tenor voice, singing very softly in the darkness of my childhood.

97

Let us cross the river and rest under the shade of the trees.

But crossing a river is not always easy, of course. There was a time when a man would have had to swim. Before Ben Colbert came along. Then, in 1858, Colbert got permission from the Chickasaw Indians to build the ferry. Colbert was an Indian himself. He ferried across the river day in and day out, night in, and night out: from Indian Territory to Texas, from Texas to Indian Territory: missionaries, cattlemen, criminals, gamblers, even the passengers on the Butterfield Stage. Ben Colbert got rich and built a spectacular house on the bluff.

(That was long ago: I think I see the dark ferryman poling his raft across Red River. Silently, through the dark of night. July, 1863. Midnight. A soldier squats on the raft and tries to sleep; his mind is beautiful with dreams of children dancing far away beneath the cottonwoods.

Lanterns swing on the corners and prick the hot blackness with their light. Travelers pay the toll: to cross the river and rest. . . .)

The railroads changed all that. The Katy came, whistling from the north, steaming across Indian Bridge and into Denison on Christmas Day, 1872. The Katy took an iron thread and tied Texas and Indian Territory together, patched them together into a piece of history. Ulysses S. Grant was president. Cowboys and Indians. Jesse James and United States marshals. New Yorkers coming out west, wearing golden watch chains and velvet spats.

The railroad cars are full of light. The chairs are covered in green velvet. Beautiful people wear white hats. They shout of victory. There are blazing chandeliers. And whiskey.

Let us cross the river and rest under the shade of the trees.

99

Red River begins in the rocky heights of the New Mexico–Texas border. It flows 1,018 miles through the Texas Panhandle, along Oklahoma's southern border, into Arkansas, then turns south through Louisiana—past Shreveport and Alexandria—to join with the Mississippi River northeast of Lettsworth.

Red River is not always red, however. Sometimes it's brown. Sometimes it's green. It all depends. They say if you stand on the bridge and if you're a beautiful person, with the right kind of music running through your body, you can lean over the railing and laugh out over the water, laugh out and clap your hands and the water will turn blue, blue as the autumn sky that's slanting over Texas. You can make Red River turn: violet as clover. That's what they say.

Let us cross the river and rest under the shade of the trees.

General Stonewall Jackson has long

been dead. And my father is dead. I've
heard the whispering of death myself.

But now: I'm on my way to Texas. I've
got me a Ford Mustang automobile and a
green silk shirt and a new pair of genuine
leather boots and I'm going into Dallas
for a weekend at the Adolphus Hotel. I'm
going to get drunk on Texas beer. I'm
going to go laughing down Commerce
Street. I'm going to go dancing with the
Texas millionaires. Oklahoma is my
home. But I like to travel to the other
shore. I'm crossing Red River once again.

(I see one single hawk lifting above the
river, sunlight on his wings, flashing out
one beautiful arc of space. Then hovering
for a beautiful moment above the bridge
—before he plunges earthward out of
sight.)

I'm crossing Red River once again. The
moment is very brief. I hold it—as long
as I dare, as long as I can—beyond the
lonely clutch of time.

Oflaggerty's Child: The Homecoming

1

Oflaggerty's child came home again.

He came when the hills were dark and turbulent with spring.

Oflaggerty's child came on a sable horse into the Osage and his eyes were deeper and he wore a lonelier smile. His fingers were dipped in dust. He came where the eagle turns in the vernal sun and the dark crows call from the sky. He came where the trails wind slowly into the hills, wind and wander like calves straying in from the pasture, wandering home to the night's corral.

He rode the trail at the canyon's edge, where the bluestem grass was sweeping, scarcely green, to the very edge of the

rock. And night came early, for the rolling hills shouldered the sun. The night
came like a herd of dark cattle up from
the canyon, cattle that were lowing and
lost, and wandering homeless over the
plain.

2

The seasons pass. To the west is the
setting sun and the endless sea. I have followed the blazing prairie and seen it fade
like a lonely trail beyond this earth and
into heaven. I have seen the curve of the
world.

I have raced on a sable horse in the
golden daylight. And I have sat quietly on
my horse, watching the sun sink into the
night. I have sat quietly on my horse while
the earth rolled, quietly, into the canyon
of darkness. And the tumbleweed has
blown in the darkness across the trail.

And I have been lonely in the west. I
have been lonely with the wind in my

hair. I have ridden my sable horse as
though I were the last of people in the
last trek across the prairies. And I have
felt as though the earth were a lost stone,
wind-swept and wandering, in a dark
journey, far from the stars. I have
mounted the desolate plateaus where the
lizards do not climb and I have surveyed
the vast wilderness of the western plains.
I have called in the night, but there was
no echo or reply. There was no sound
but only silence, until it was broken by
the neighing horse, suddenly frightened.

3

I have come home again. I have ridden
by the northern hill where the Osage
chiefs are sleeping beneath white stones
that flash in the setting sun. I pause at the
foot of the hill, and in the fading light I
lift my eyes in sad and brief salute. I
speak to them. Chief Bacon Rind. Chief
Lookout. And other mighty names.

4

Many men lie down on the earth and look at the stars.

At night when the stars are clear, men lie down on the prairie and look at the sky, and the rolling of the universe amazes them, and they shudder with loneliness.

Summer night, winter night. They lie thinking that the wind blows across them and rustles the tall grass around them, but soon there will be only the wind and the still night. Many men lie and look at the stars and think that we are like rocks that crumble and fade away. Even the trees shall fall and the hills shall fall and the earth be split asunder.

But none shall pass as quickly as Oflaggerty's child—the counter of stars and the herder of cattle. None shall linger so briefly—as the rider of horses and the hunter of eagles.